Great Events

The BATTLE of BRITAIN

Written and Illustrated by Gillian Clements

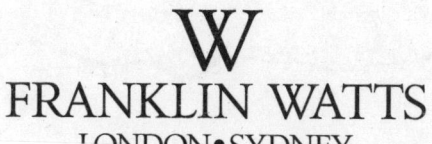

W
FRANKLIN WATTS
LONDON • SYDNEY

This edition 2014

First published in 2003 by
Franklin Watts
338 Euston Road
London NW1 3BH

Franklin Watts Australia
Level 17/207 Kent Street
Sydney NSW 2000

Copyright © 2002 Gillian Clements

The right of the author to be identified
as the author of this work has been asserted.

ISBN 978 1 4451 3123 8

Dewey Decimal Classification Number: 940.53

A CIP catalogue record for this book
is available from the British Library.

Series editor: Rachel Cooke
Historical consultant: Claire Edwards

Printed in Great Britain

Franklin Watts is a division of Hachette Children's
Books, an Hachette UK company.
www.hachette.co.uk

The BATTLE of BRITAIN

It was June 1940. Europe was at war – the Second World War. The strong German army had forced the Allies – Britain, France and Belgium – to retreat to the town of Dunkirk on the French coast. Now there was nowhere to go but the sea.

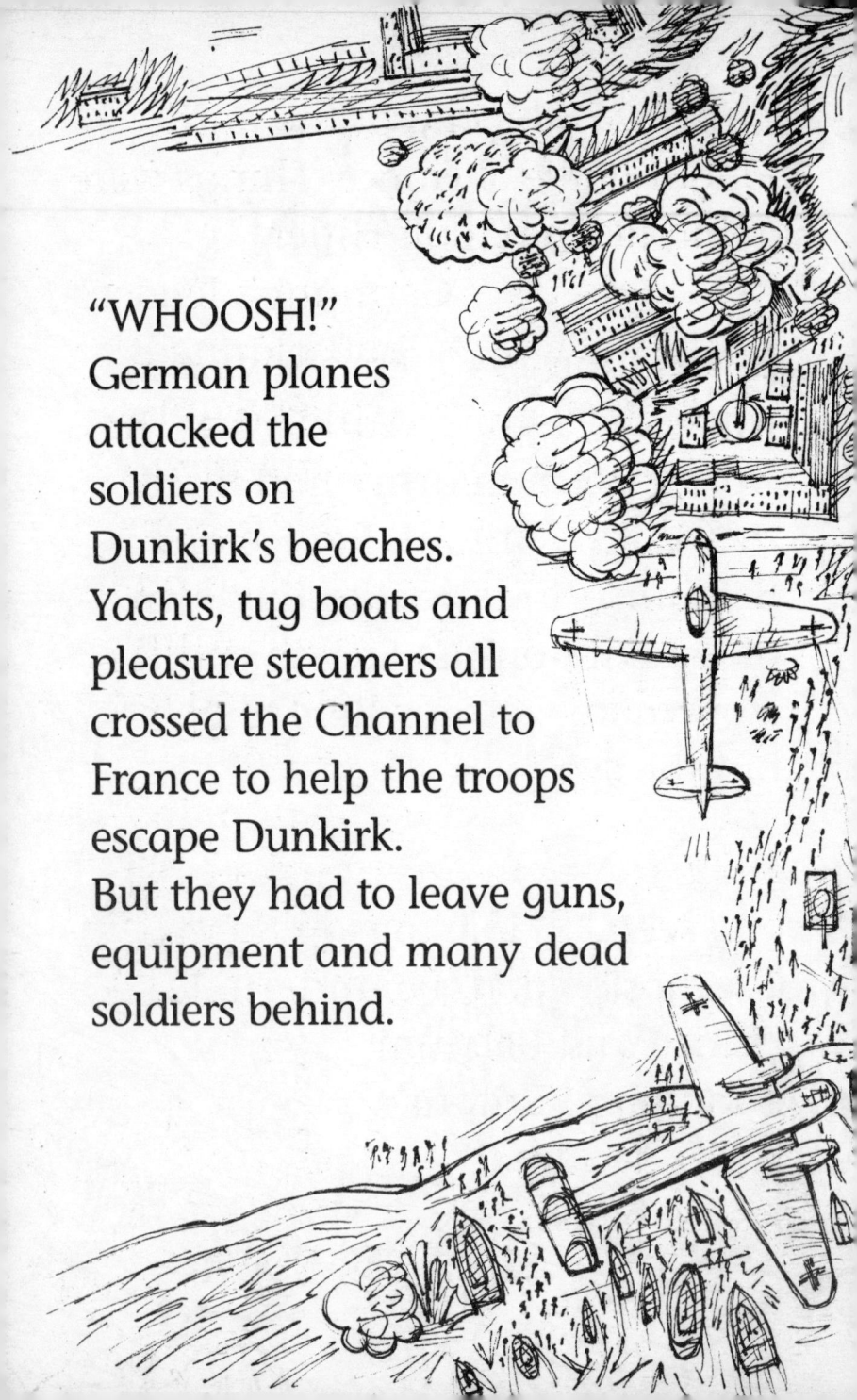

"WHOOSH!"
German planes attacked the soldiers on Dunkirk's beaches. Yachts, tug boats and pleasure steamers all crossed the Channel to France to help the troops escape Dunkirk.
But they had to leave guns, equipment and many dead soldiers behind.

This was the end of the hard-fought Battle of France. Things were going just as Adolf Hitler,

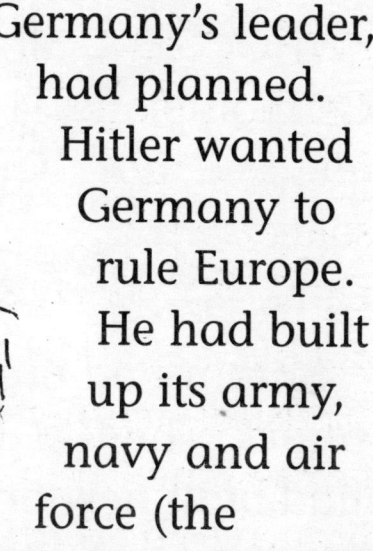

Germany's leader, had planned. Hitler wanted Germany to rule Europe. He had built up its army, navy and air force (the Luftwaffe) and, in 1939, the Germans attacked. No one seemed able to stop them. Czechoslovakia, Poland, Holland, France and Belgium had fallen. Britain, Hitler declared, would be next.

BRITAIN

GERMANY

POLAND

FRANCE

CZECHO-SLOVAKIA

ITALY

Britain had prepared for an attack. The RAF (Royal Air Force) had built new and faster planes – Hurricanes, Spitfires, Defiants. British scientists had developed radar, too. Amazingly, it could detect things in the air long before you could see them. Radar stations built along the British coast could warn the RAF when German planes were on their way.

On 10th July 1940, Dover radar warned: "Mass of German fighters and bombers over French coast!"

"SCRAMBLE! SCRAMBLE!" The order came through for British fighters to take to the air. They flew towards the German planes. *"Ratatat!"* Guns fired as the battle for the skies began.

On this first attack, the Germans came off worse, losing many more planes than the British.

Let us brace ourselves that, if the British Empire and the Commonwealth last for a thousand years, men will say, 'This was their finest hour.'

Yet Prime Minister Winston Churchill prepared the country for the struggle ahead.

On 16th July, Hitler announced his plans: "I have decided to begin to prepare for an invasion."

Hitler's Luftwaffe started to bomb British ships and aircraft factories. Unknown to Hitler, Britain had cracked the Luftwaffe's top-secret code using the "Enigma" machine – so they found out many of the Germans' secret plans.

The British defended their land against possible German invaders. Tank traps and fortified pillboxes sprang up in the countryside. Local Defence Volunteers laid barbed wire on beaches and cliffs. To confuse any invaders, street names and signposts were taken down. "CARELESS TALK COSTS LIVES!" posters warned. Spies could be anywhere...

Across the Channel, Germany's huge airfleets were ready to attack. They had 316 dive-bombers and over 1,000 of long-range bombers and 1,000 fighters. The Germans were confident, but knew the British would not give up easily.

11

For weeks, air battles were fought above the Channel.

The New York Times

Sometimes the planes were so high they looked like tiny specks. The battles raged so furiously that it was impossible to keep track of the planes that fell.

German Stuka bombers and British Defiants struggled in skirmishes called dogfights. Protecting convoys of British ships in the Channel, Defiant after Defiant plunged into the sea.

The German army continued making its invasion plans. "We will land in Sussex and Kent," its generals told Hitler.

"We must win England's skies first!" Hitler declared. Although by July, Germany had already lost over twice as many planes as Britain, Goering, the Luftwaffe's High Commander, was confident.

The Luftwaffe can conquer England by itself!

In early August, Goering decided to bomb the radar towers first. "CRASH!" Bombs fell on the radar towers at Pevensey, Dover and Rye. "CRUMP!" German long-range guns were fired from France and killed people in Dover.

We'll test the RADAR, now we've bombed them.

14

The Germans sent another wave of bombers and fighters. Some dive-bombed ships near the Thames. Others flew west to attack the navy at Portsmouth. The rest targeted England's airfields in the South. On the ground, engineers worked frantically to repair the radar towers.

15

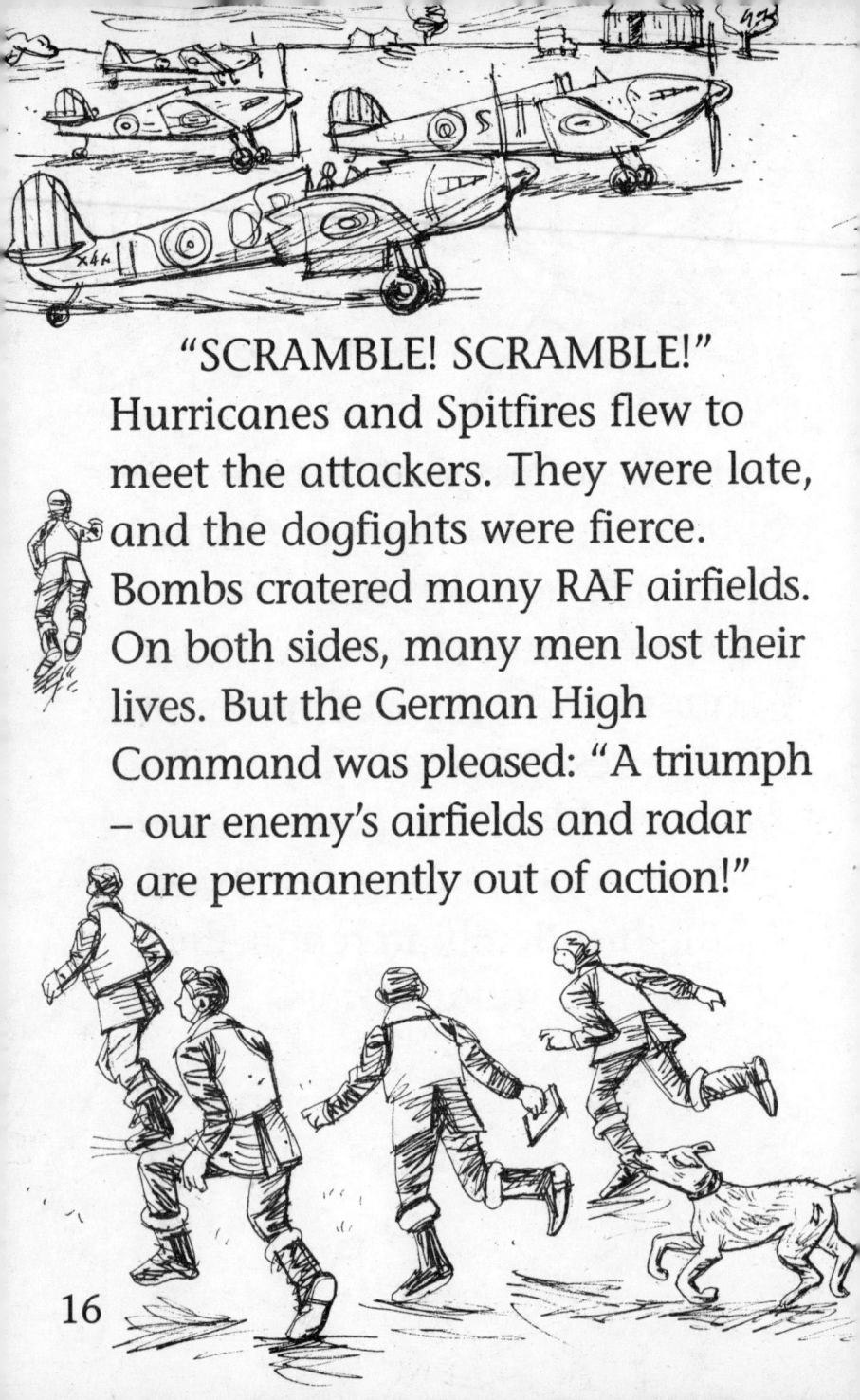

"SCRAMBLE! SCRAMBLE!" Hurricanes and Spitfires flew to meet the attackers. They were late, and the dogfights were fierce. Bombs cratered many RAF airfields. On both sides, many men lost their lives. But the German High Command was pleased: "A triumph – our enemy's airfields and radar are permanently out of action!"

16

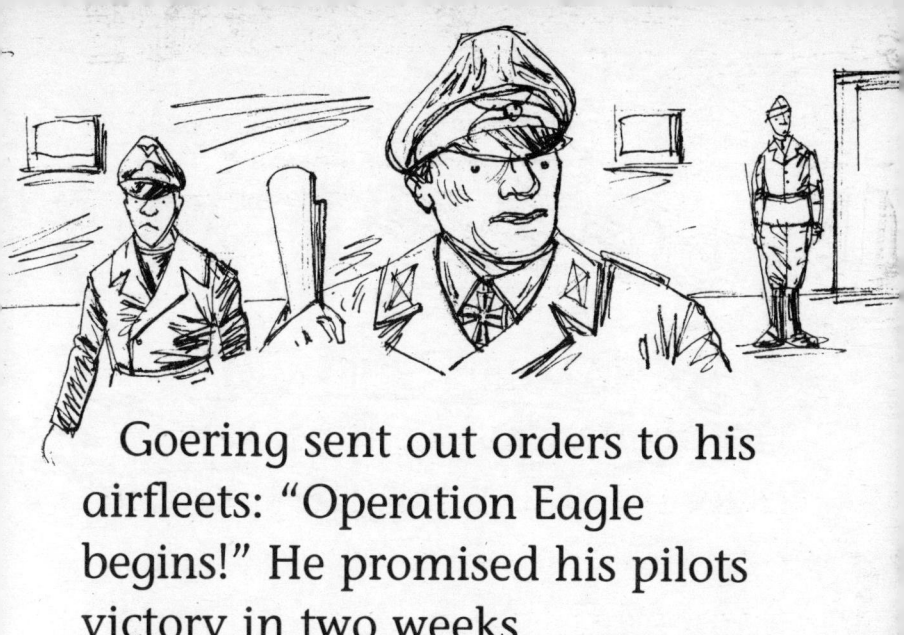

Goering sent out orders to his airfleets: "Operation Eagle begins!" He promised his pilots victory in two weeks...

13th August – Goering's Eagle Day – began grey in France, and cloudy over England. But, already at 4,000 metres, a wave of Luftwaffe bombers had begun its flight to England.

London

ENGLAND Dover

Calais

FRANCE

Rye

Pevensey

English Channel

17

The weather closed in. "CALL OFF THE ATTACK!" radioed Goering. The Messerschmitt fighter escort turned back, but his bombers carried on.

British radar picked them up. "BANDITS OVER THE THAMES!" 74 Squadron met the unprotected bombers – and sent five German planes crashing into the Kent hills. Six more were badly damaged.

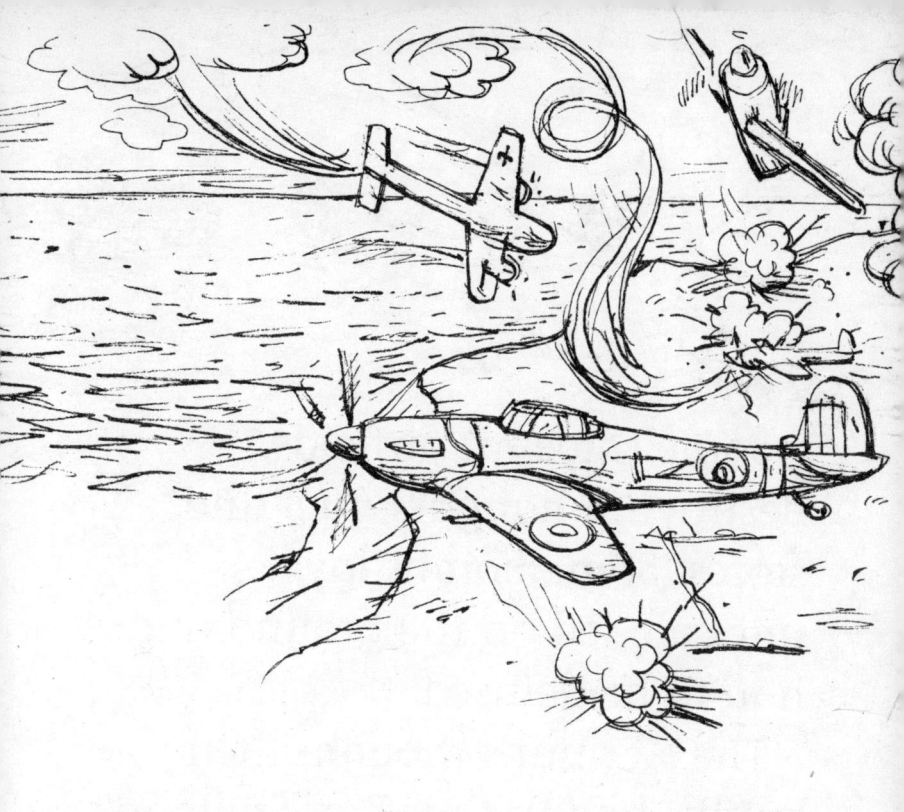

Goering was furious. He sent a second huge attack. British fighters, greatly outnumbered, flew to meet them. Children excitedly scanned the sky and watched the Spitfires give chase to the German bombers.

Some raids hit airfields, destroying hangars, fuel and stores. Some bombs lay unexploded on the ground and had to be defused.

The Germans thought their bombs had put most of England's radar and southern airfields out of use. They did not see how quickly they were repaired.

13th August, Eagle Day, was long. One German attack after another approached the English coast. They bombed docks in Southampton and aircraft factories in Birmingham. Many civilians died, and the RAF lost over 30 fighter planes... but the Luftwaffe had not won the day.

Hitler was furious.

This is one of the greatest days in history!

The cloud and showers of late August brought RAF pilots a welcome rest. British airmen relaxed, as did Poles, Czechs, Belgians and Frenchmen who had fled the German invasions. There were Irish and American flyers nearby, and pilots from Australia, New Zealand, Canada, Africa and Jamaica. All enjoyed the calm while they could.

The bad weather meant there was time enough for repairs, but too little to train young pilots. Between 8th and 17th August, the RAF had lost 154 flyers – often the best, most experienced men. New ones had little practice and a lot to learn.

I fired my guns once, into a cloud.

Though it was a black week for Goering, he kept to his plans. "Continue to attack their airfields!" he ordered the Luftwaffe.

British squadron leaders knew what to do. They flew at the German bombers and fighters, all guns firing, then swerved at the very last moment. A split second too long and they would collide and explode. It was dangerous and exhausting.

My nerves were in ribbons... I was scared stiff that one day I would pull out and avoid combat.

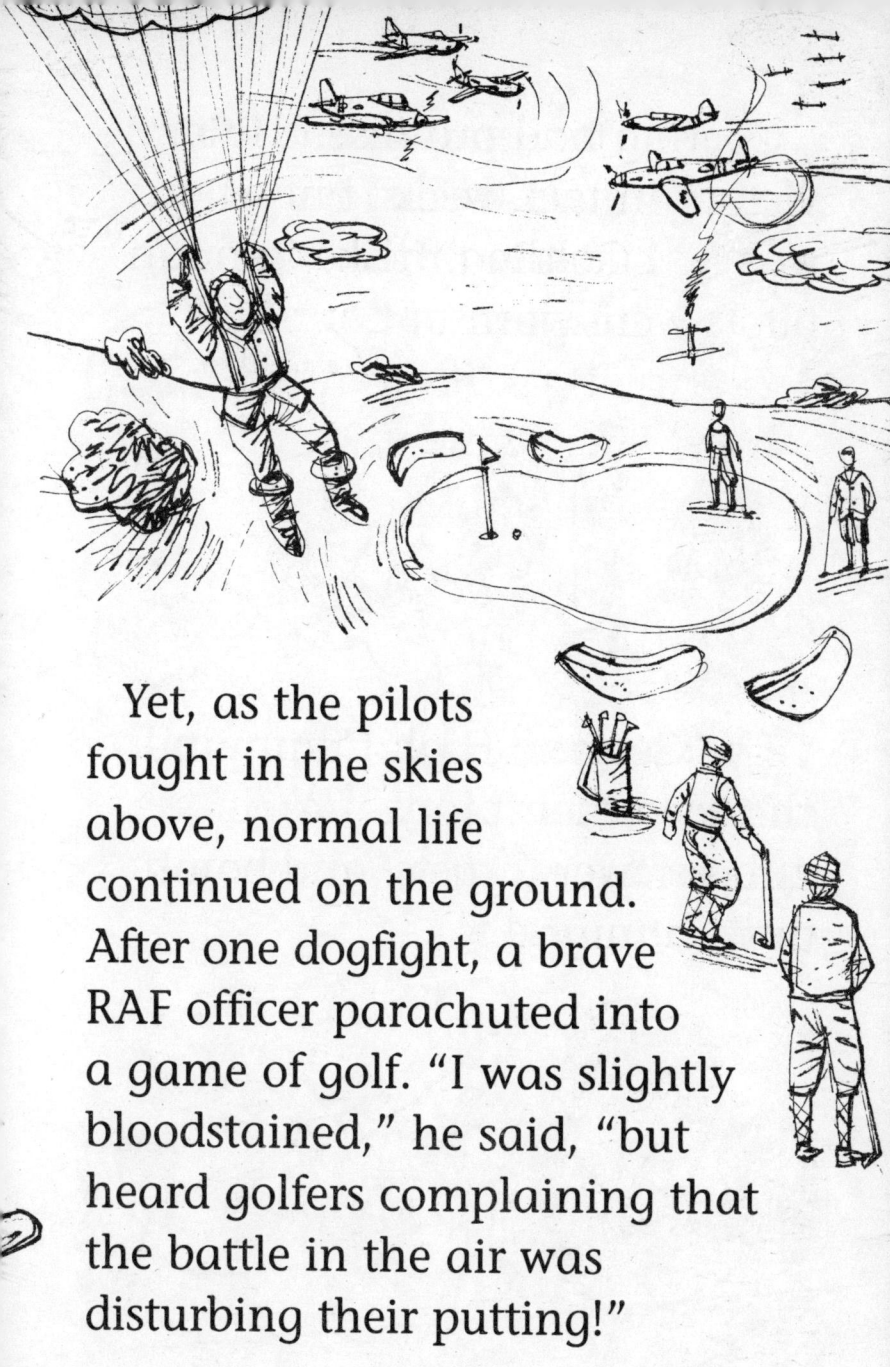

Yet, as the pilots fought in the skies above, normal life continued on the ground. After one dogfight, a brave RAF officer parachuted into a game of golf. "I was slightly bloodstained," he said, "but heard golfers complaining that the battle in the air was disturbing their putting!"

Goering had promised Hitler victory in two weeks, but where was it? Like the British, German pilots were worn out.

Utter exhaustion from the English operations had set in.

The German High Command changed their plans. "We'll attack fewer targets, and bomb them at night!"

On 24th August, what became known as the Blitz began. The Luftwaffe concentrated on city targets – London, Portsmouth, and cities in the Midlands and North West. Fires burnt out of control.

Britain lost more and more planes. How much longer could the country survive?

"GERMANS JETTISON BOMBS OVER LONDON! The Barbican bombed! Finsbury and Islington, too!" Churchill was very angry. But these raids changed the Battle of Britain. Ever since Eagle Day, the British had been reconsidering *their* plans, too. They decided to send fewer squadrons out to fight – and bomb the Germans instead!

We can put a raid against Berlin in a day.

Ground engineers loaded the British Wellington and Hampden bombers as quickly as they could.

"BERLIN BOMBED. CIVILIANS KILLED!" The RAF attacked for three nights, and some bombs had missed their factory targets. The Berliners could not believe it had happened.

"Now I WILL destroy London!" Hitler fumed. "Since they attack our cities, we shall wipe out theirs."

He drew up his plans. German planes would create terror and chaos in London, then the invasion could begin. He even set an invasion date: 21st September...

When we have air superiority over Southern England and the English Channel.

On 7th September, a huge air armada of German bombers and Messerschmitt escorts took off. The line of squadrons was over 30 kilometres long! Smiling, Goering watched them fly towards the English coast.

In the RAF operations room, controllers plotted the armada's progress on a great table. Once again, Britain's tired pilots took to the air.

Outnumbered ten to one, Spitfires and Hurricanes tore into German bombers. British pilots and anti-aircraft fire shot some down. But the planes kept coming.

"CRASH!" The East End rattled to huge explosions – hundreds of Londoners died that day.

There was more bombing at night. London's railways took the brunt. "At 9 p.m.," said Russia's ambassador, "there began a kind of strange roar. Then we saw high tongues of flame." One attack targeted Buckingham Palace and the King.

London – and other cities – lay in ruins. But Dowding, Britain's Air Chief Marshal, was relieved. The Germans had made a mistake. If they had carried on bombing Britain's airfields and planes, the RAF's air defences may have collapsed. By bombing London, the Germans gave the RAF a chance to recover.

However, the code breakers had worked out some frightening news: it looked as if Germany was planning to invade soon.

"INVASION IMMINENT! ALL TROOPS TO BATTLE STATIONS!" Britain's High Command ordered.

In a panic, soldiers blew up bridges to delay an invasion, and Britain's church bells rang. But it was a false alarm.

And still, night after night, London's Blitz raged on. German planes dropped deadly bombs... but no invasion fleet sailed.

11th September was a very bad day. "GERMAN BOMBERS SIGHTED! SCRAMBLE!"

Sixteen British squadrons
climbed into the clearing skies,
till the air was a crowd of planes.
Spitfires and Hurricanes attacked
to break the bombers' formations
– but still London's City district
and docks were hit.

The night's work killed hundreds of Londoners and pilots. More British planes were lost than German. In Britain, everyone held their breath. Surely Hitler would invade soon.

But the German leader delayed. "The Luftwaffe still has not mastered the skies. We need one final deadly blow!" He chose 15th September.

Sunday 15th September began sunny and fine. In England, Churchill watched at Fighter Command's HQ. The radar operators warned of another massive German air attack... Ten British squadrons were airborne before the Germans had reached the English coast.

39

The Germans still undervalued Britain's radar. Squadron after squadron were scrambling from all over the country. There had never been so many aloft at one time – and all before midday. Hurricanes and Spitfires hurriedly climbed beyond 5,000 metres… then the combat began.

"BUZZ THEM, ATTACK HEAD ON!" squadron leaders ordered.

Furiously they attacked, until the German bombers' nerves and formations crumbled. The Germans were exhausted and turning for home in a hurry. A new wave arrived, slow and disorganised and the Messerschmitts, low on fuel, left the bombers behind defenceless. Now they turned tail too as 150 Spitfires and Hurricanes screamed in.

ATTACK! ATTACK!

For two years I have been told, 'Just one last effort!' But it is never so.

It was like a miracle!

"We have shot down 183 for a loss of under 40!" Churchill's beaming Private Secretary exaggerated. Luftwaffe losses were actually nearer 60, but it was clear their spirit was broken.

And from that day on, every 15th September was called Battle of Britain Day.

Hitler postponed his invasion of England. By the end of October 1940, the Battle of Britain was over. The Luftwaffe had failed to win control of Britain's skies. Hitler would send no more mass attacks. Instead, he set his sights on Russia.

The Second World War carried on. There were more bombing raids. The Americans joined the fighting too and eventually, in 1945, Germany was defeated. But after the Battle of Britain, Hitler never tried to invade again.

The radar operators, the code breakers, the engineers and the RAF fighter pilots had saved Britain. As Winston Churchill said: "Never in the field of human conflict was so much owed by so many to so few."

Timeline

1933 Hitler becomes Germany's leader.

1934 Churchill warns Parliament about Germany's strong air force.

1935 Robert Watson Watt designs and builds radar equipment.

1938 Germany prepares for war.

1939 **3rd September** Britain and France declare war on Germany.

1940 **May** Britain forms Home Guard to defend against an invasion.
29th May–4th June British and other troops evacuated from Dunkirk, after Belgium falls to the Germans.
17th June Germany wins Battle of France.
10th July Battle of Britain begins.
16th July Hitler announces his plan to invade Britain.
25th July German bombers sink British ships in the Channel.
8th August 2nd phase of the Battle of Britain begins. Heavy fighting follows in the skies above Britain. Germans target air force bases.

13th August Goering's Eagle Day.
19th–23rd August Bad weather brings a break in the fighting.
24th August 3rd phase of the Battle of Britain. British towns and cities hit.
25th August RAF bomb Berlin at night in response to London bombs.
7th September 4th phase of the Battle of Britain. Heavy bombing of London begins. Invasion of Britain planned for 21st September.
15th September "Battle of Britain Day". Largest ever bombing of London and the South. Radar warns British of the attack. The British are outnumbered but win the Battle.
17th September Hitler postpones invasion of Britain.
30th September Last daytime bombing raid on London.
1st October 5th phase of the Battle of Britain begins with attacks on London at night.
16th October Autumn weather brings an end to the bombing raids. The Battle of Britain is soon over.

1945 **May** Germany surrenders. The war in Europe is over.

Glossary

Allies The countries who agreed to fight together against Germany in the Second World War.

Blitz Bomb attacks by aircraft on a city. From *Blitzkrieg*, the German for *lightning war*.

Civilian A person not in the armed forces.

Convoy Vehicles travelling together.

Defence Volunteers People in the "Home Guard", set up to defend Britain against invasion in the Second World War.

Enigma machine Machine used by the British to crack German codes during the war.

Fighter escort Aircraft that travel in convoy with bomber planes to protect them.

Fortified Made stronger against an attack.

Hangar Building where aircraft are kept.

HQ Abbreviation for headquarters.

Luftwaffe The German air force.

Pillbox A small concrete fort.

Radar A way of discovering the position of something through using radio signals.

Scramble To prepare for immediate action.

Squadron Part of one of the armed forces.